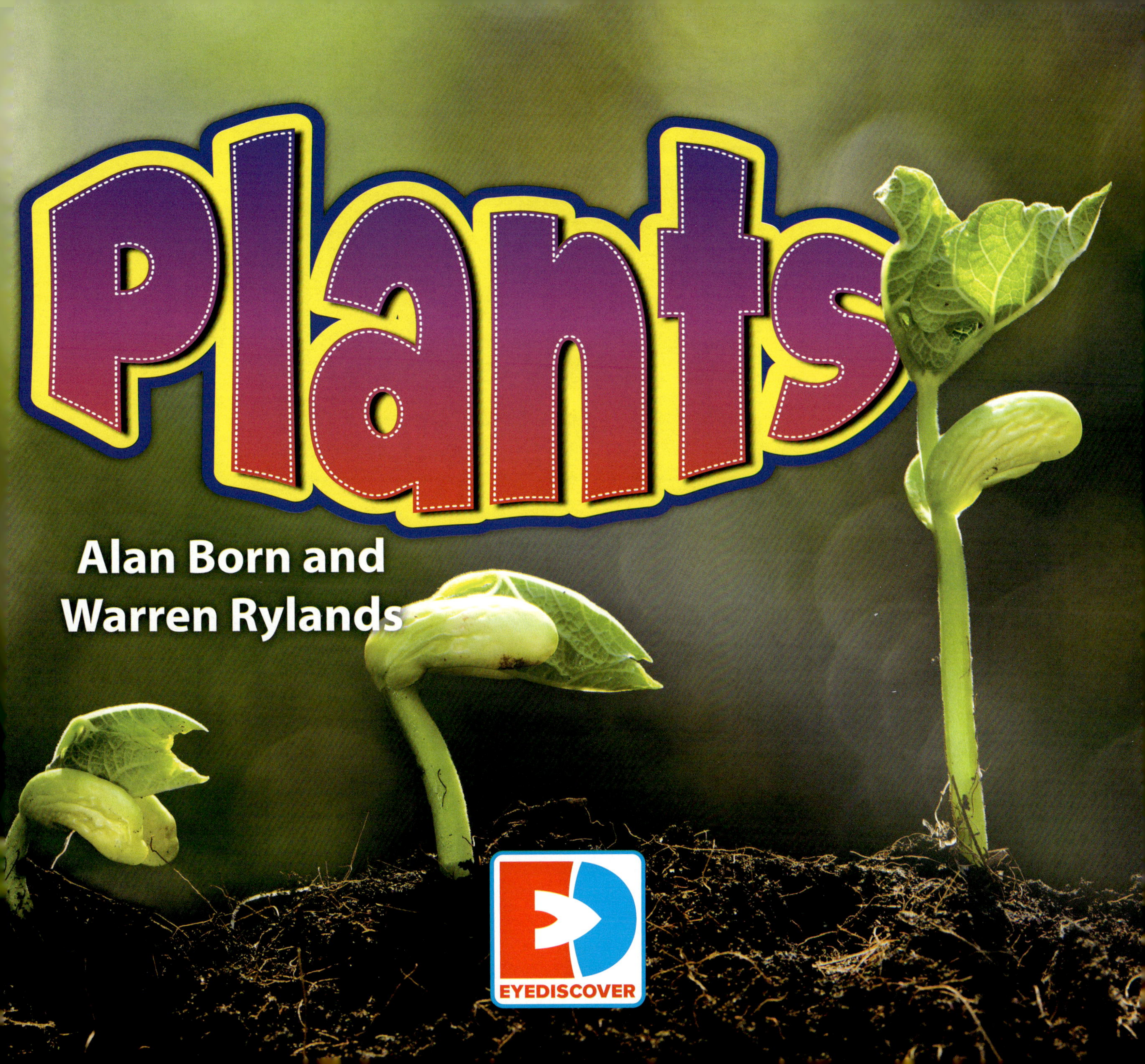
Plants
Alan Born and
Warren Rylands
EYEDISCOVER

Go to www.eyediscover.com and enter this book's unique code.

BOOK CODE

AVS69289

EYEDISCOVER brings you optic readalongs that support active learning.

Published by AV² by Weigl
350 5th Avenue, 59th Floor New York, NY 10118
Website: www.eyediscover.com

Library of Congress Control Number: 2018954252

ISBN 978-1-4896-8003-7 (hardcover)

Printed in Brainerd, Minnesota, United States
1 2 3 4 5 6 7 8 9 0 22 21 20 19 18

082018
120917

Project Coordinator: John Willis
Designer: Mandy Christiansen

Weigl acknowledges Alamy, Shutterstock, and iStock as the primary image suppliers for this title.

EYEDISCOVER provides enriched content, optimized for tablet use, that supplements and complements this book. EYEDISCOVER books strive to create inspired learning and engage young minds in a total learning experience.

Your EYEDISCOVER Optic Readalongs come alive with...

Audio
Listen to the entire book read aloud.

Video
High resolution videos turn each spread into an optic readalong.

OPTIMIZED FOR
- TABLETS
- WHITEBOARDS
- COMPUTERS
- AND MUCH MORE!

In this book, you will learn about

- how they change
- what makes them grow
- how they spread

and much more!

Inside a seed is
a tiny plant.

The plant grows until it sprouts as a seedling.

Seeds and seedlings need water to grow. Sunlight and soil also help them grow.

10

A plant has roots that help it get water and food.

The stem stretches up from the roots. It carries water and food to the leaves.

Some plants have flowers. Part of the flower makes tiny grains called pollen.

Pollen will stick to an insect when it lands on the flower.

Insects carry pollen from flower to flower.

A flower uses pollen to make new seeds. These seeds fall and grow into new plants.

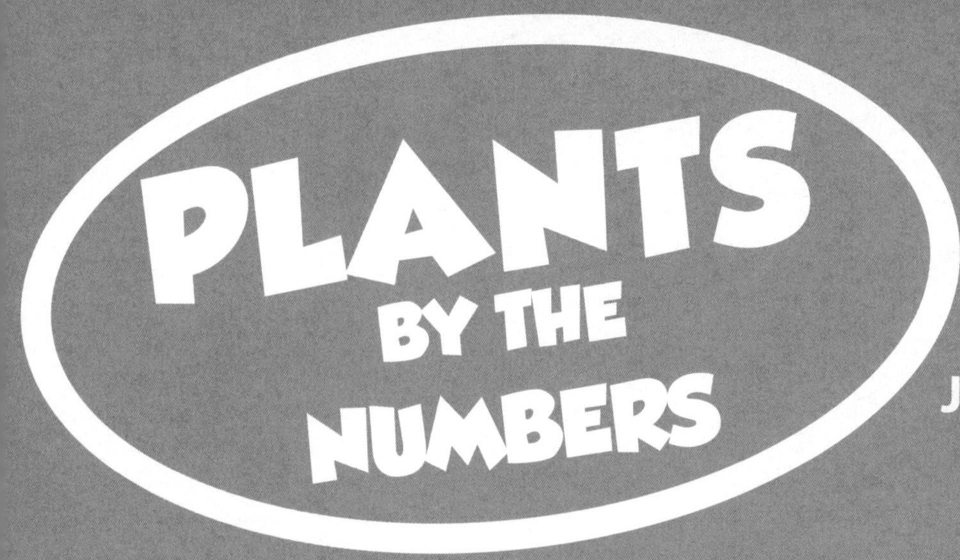

Just **one female bee** can visit about **50,000** blueberry **flowers** in her lifetime.

Rafflesia flowers can be nearly **3 feet** (1 meter) across. That is **as big** as an **umbrella**.

The average **strawberry** is covered in about 200 **tiny fruits**.

Moonflowers may have gotten their name because they look like the moon and **bloom at night.**

The **tallest** sunflower ever grown was **30 feet** (9 meters) tall. That is about **twice as tall** as a **giraffe.**

Dandelion seeds are **shaped** like **parachutes** so they can fly.

KEY WORDS

Research has shown that as much as 65 percent of all written material published in English is made up of 300 words. These 300 words cannot be taught using pictures or learned by sounding them out. They must be recognized by sight. This book contains 37 common sight words to help young readers improve their reading fluency and comprehension. This book also teaches young readers several important content words, such as proper nouns. These words are paired with pictures to aid in learning and improve understanding.

Page	Sight Words First Appearance
4	a, is, plant
7	as, grows, it, the, until
8	also, and, help, need, them, to, water
11	food, get, has, that
12	from, leaves, up
15	have, makes, of, part, some
16	an, lands, on, when, will
19	carry
20	into, new, these, uses

Page	Content Words First Appearance
4	seed
7	seedling
8	soil, sunlight
11	roots
12	stem
15	flowers, grains, pollen
16	insect

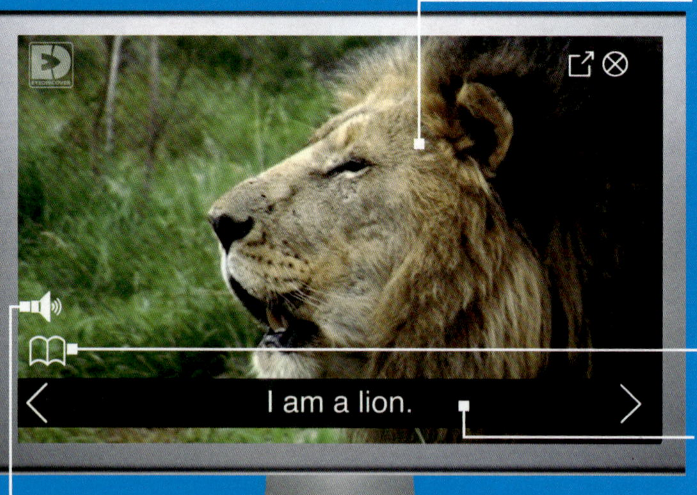

Watch
Video content brings each page to life.

Browse
Thumbnails make navigation simple.

Read
Follow along with text on the screen.

Listen
Hear each page read aloud.

Go to www.eyediscover.com and enter this book's unique code.

BOOK CODE

AVS69289